The Heart Speaks

Also by Samantha Jo Gabardi

Whispers of a Silent Heart

The Heart Speaks

a collection of poetry and prose

by Samantha Jo Gabardi

Independently Published

United States

Copyright © by Samantha Jo Gabardi
All rights reserved.

No part of this book may be reproduced in any form or by any electronic or mechanical means including information storage and retrieval systems, without permission in writing from the author. The only exception is for instances of cited quotations and book reviews or articles written about the book and/or author.

ISBN-9798699509829

First Printing December 2020
Independently Published

Printed in The United States of America

I would just like to take a moment to thank a few special people for their help.
First of all, a huge, heartfelt thank you to my friend, Charlene Benoit. This woman has been such a huge help to me, and this book wouldn't even be here if it weren't for her dedication in helping to walk me through the process! She is a writer and Author herself of many wonderful books,which can be found on Amazon. Some of those books are: In The Hearts of Gods, Monsters, and Men, and Blood Tears and Coffee Rings.
I hope you check her out!
Love to you, Charlene!
I would also like to give a special thanks to my family, for their support, encouragement, love, and patience with me as I spent many long hours in writing.
I love you guys,always!
To the readers of my words, you keep me going, much appreciation to you all!
And most importantly, I thank God for making all things possible, for strength, hope, and helping me navigate through life and to the importance of things, which is love.

For those who know what
it is to bleed but still
find magic in everything..

one of the first prayers
i ever sent up was:
God, let me see the
world through your eyes,
and please give me the
ability to withstand
what i see.' –
i have been weeping
rivers, ever since..

this is my heart,
and sometimes,
i don 't wear her
so well–
but she is mine,
and i love her. .

the walls of my
heart
are covered in
drafts
i hastily
scribble to myself..

i am but a stranger
to this awful
and beautiful world.
no matter how much i try
to fit in, i just don 't.
i 'm too dark, too deep,
and too much do i weep;
my wings have all been
dipped in black,
and i hold darkness
as a friend−
but still, in all this,
i find the beauty of it all:
i was only ever meant to
stand up, stand out ,
and show others the beauty
in the fall. .

there's a certain beauty that
comes with weeping:
kind of like the way
the sky exists after a
hard rain, when the clouds
begin to clear off and the
blue just kind of stands
out at its most brightest. .

that's the thing with
broken souls—
they love too hard,
and the world just isn't
ready for that..

the rain holds a story
and it 's as beautiful
as the stories each
teardrop tells. .

people say they want real,
but in reality, they don't-
they '11 accept
your smile, your laugh. .
but give them your
whole truth:
the fears, your bones
when they splinter and
begin to crack, and they'11
head for the hills;
because for some reason,
people are afraid of
things that bleed..

she was raised in a world
that was conditioned:
one in which love was
not given, unless she
lived by a certain set
of rules.
so please understand,
that when her tears fall
like rain and you attempt
to pull her into your
comforting arms,
she may push you away —
not because she doesn't
want that, she very much
does, but because she feels
undeserving of that love.
in those moments,
hold her still..

when the right one comes
along, you won't have
to stumble across your
words in an attempt to
explain your soul—
they will simply. .
understand

she scares you because
you don't want to feel
ANYTHING,
and she makes you feel
EVERYTHING..

learn to live in the
moment,
because that 's all
there really is. .

you have me—
no matter what may come,
I' M YOURS. .

loving you comes so
naturally now,
like breathing. .

i shall never forget how
beautifully you colored
my world –
and i will love you
FOREVER, and EVER,
and EVER. .

..and EVER..

..and he asked her,
'what's the most beautiful
poem you've ever read? '

..to which she replied,
'YOU'..

love her without words. .

don't get so busy being
distracted by life
that you forget
to enjoy it;
because, all to often,
the best days of your
life are happening right
in front of you,
and you don't really
realize that until they
become a
MEMORY..

love is–
a constant choosing. .

if only i could be
as tiny as the
fairies and ride
on butterfly wings. .

oh, the bravery of
ink-stained
hearts,
and paper souls..

i woke up with the
love of my life
standing before me—
with eyes bright enough
to light up the entire
midnight sky,
a heart strong enough to
hold even the darkest
of souls, and a love
that had the ability to
bring smiles to the
world around her. .
i woke up today with
the love of my life
standing before me—
and she. . was me. .

a love so sacred,
that even the flowers
🥀 bow their heads,
and the
butterflies stop to stare. .

gently she walks through
life, leaving flowers
of kindness
behind as she goes—
hoping that, one day,
someone might pick up
the scent,
and follow it to her heart. .

there's a pup living
in my mind that
likes to play fetch–
and when i throw
him a stick,
he always manages
to bring
something back. .

Chapter Thirty-Seven

still seeking human kindness..

there are some people
that you will spend a
lifetime trying to
explain your soul to,
and then,
there are those who will
simple fall into it
without any words needed–
hang on to
the ones that fall..

sometimes, love is like
a huge game of
hide-and-go-seek,
where you 're
the one hiding,
and everyone else
has gone home. .

and she would wear his
soul
in her hair,
like a freshly-plucked
wildflower..

if you press your ear
to the door
of my heart and
breathe, ever so quietly,
you can hear us
laughing, talking, and holding
one another under the stars.
at midnight. .

come, my love,
let us go to a quiet
place where
we can sip our coffee,
read our books to little
inquisitive animals,
and watch the creatures
of the forest
gather 'round to quietly
listen –
come, my love..

close your eyes,
darling,
and listen to the
gentle whispers of
my soul. .

gently,
i dipped the tips of
my fingers into
the river of his soul
and watched as he
rippled an
unending circle of love. .

tell me, my love,
just how your colors
grow—
i wish for nothing
more than an
understanding of how you,
so beautifully,
bleed the rainbow. .

don't just tell her
that you love her,
show her—
make her feel it
deep within her bones. .

i found a home in
your heart ,
where my spirit
is restless no more—
where waves crash gently,
like thunder,
against the distant shore..

sometimes, i wonder
just how many storms
your eyes
must have faced,
before they became
so kind? ?

speak your truth,
dear soul,
even if it makes people
uncomfortable..

never loose
your inner child,
never forfeit
your imagination,
and never loose
your ability to find
magic and peace in the
smallest of things..

you deserve a love
that 's patient
with your heart,
one that 's loving
and nurturing
to your soul –
after everything you ' ve
made it through,
never settle for anything
less than
that type of kindness. .

it wasn 't that i needed
to hear i was beautiful ,
it just sounded so good
echoing from your lips..

..and he had a certain
way about him—
always making each day
more adventurous
than the last. .

someone once asked me
what love was and
all i could think about
was you. .

i love the way my heart
curves
around his smile. .

it never took much
to make her smile:
a blanket under the stars,
a hand-in-hand walk by
the water's edge,
maybe even a cup of
coffee on the front
porch of a
misty morning. .
things like that–
she was a simple girl,
who fell in love
with simple things,
and that was
just too damn lovely
to ever let go..

of all the
beautiful roses
in the garden,
he picked me,
a wildflower. .

I NEED YOU
like i need the green,
cool grass
beneath my bare feet,
like a gentle heartbeat–
like the warmth
of the lifeblood,
running through my veins,
or the soft gentle rain
that soothes,
I NEED YOU..

PEACE IS:
a quiet morning,
a warm cup of coffee
on a dreary,
Sunday morning,
a gentle, cool wind,
brushing my face,
old books, and..
YOU

poetry is limited when
it comes to
that sacred smile
shining
from your eyes. .

casting my wishes upon
the breeze,
in hopes that they find
their way to you. .

you are. .

all things lovely. .

sometimes,
i sit and wonder if
we're all just a corpse
walking around,
just a bag of bones,
unaware of our state
of death—
where deja vu
is but a simple reminder
of a life already lived? ?

late nights,
his arms wrapped around
me from behind,
pointing out every
constellation
in the midnight sky–

THAT

if you have
the ability to
face yourself,
you can face anyone..

we spend our whole lives
looking for love,
only to discover
that it 's been
inside of us, all along–
focus your attention
on that. . on your hopes,
your dreams, and the
things that inspire you
and eventually,
when you're not
paying attention,
love will find you. .

..and i hope that life
brings you a someone
who melts your heart
with love,
a person who inspires
you so much, that they
bring your soul
to its knees–
and i hope when life
brings you this someone,
they hold you tight,
and never let you go. .

too many times,
i watch
as beautiful hearts are
cast by the wayside,
taken advantage of ,
and left alone
to bleed..

real connections
are about as rare
as intelligence,
nowadays. .

..and sometimes,
there are no words,
just an exchange of energy,
speaking its own language,
and only known by us. .

words are nice,
but what my soul craves
are the actions that
BACK IT UP..

embrace each other
like it 's the last time,
EVERY TIME..

she just wanted
to feel wanted
by a soul who couldn't
forget her. .

i don 't believe i've ever
met anyone more lovely
than him,
nor will i ever again.
he is a once in a lifetime
kind of love,
may i never
take him for granted. .

the only thing i ever
asked love for,
was a best friend.
one who saw the ache
in my heart,
and still chose
to stay, anyways. .

there will come a
TIME
when the only thing
you'll want from them—
is more
TIME..

there are some people
in this world
that have a way of
pulling magic and adventure
out of everything
that they do,
and if you just so happen
to run across that
type of soul,
hang on tight
and never let go. .

i find it so sad
that some people
would rather leave
and miss out on a
good thing,
than to stay
and work through
something simple..

i think we're all
just looking for someone
who will hold us until
we breathe our last. .

wait for the one that
wants to learn the
rhythm of your soul ,
the one who sees the
beauty you miss in yourself,
and reminds you of it
every single day—
and when the day comes
that you are graced
with their presence,
do the same
and waltz with them,
soul to soul,
until the very end of time. .

give me that old-fashioned
love, the kind everyone
dreams of-
with cotton-candy kisses atop
the ferris wheel,
peaceful sun-gazes on
the rowboat of a
middays afternoon. .
the kind of love that
takes you on a picnic in a
field of nowhere,
the kind where the guy
asks dad for my hand. .
give me the love that
still opens doors, slides out
chairs, and hides in the
backseat of that old
coupe de ville,
giving neck-nibbles when
we should be watching the
picture show instead.
i want the love where
food is brought to us
on roller skates, and the
lover throws rocks at my
window, quietly from my
mother ' s front gate-
yes, that kind of love.
an old fashioned love,
where giving up wasn 't
an option, respect and
admiration were a given,
and the memories
grew them together- in love. .

i could say 'i love you'
a million times
and it would never
be enough–
because there is something
greater than that,
and that,
is where i love you. .

beautiful
is the one that holds on,
when everyone else
is letting go. .

don 't wait for moments
to come,
make them
while you can—
because life goes faster
than you realize
and in the end,
it will be the memories
that hold you. .

..and just like that,
you showed up–
and if that wasn't enough,
you stayed..
and that's all i ever
really asked for..

i watched
as our pup climbed up
on the bed, laying down
on the old
t-shirt you wore
last night ,
and i totally understood him—
i miss you like that when
you ' re away. .

freedom lies in
not giving a fuck,
but i do—
and that has always
been my tragedy..

bring not thy love
unless thou art willing
to stay. .

i find that the best
way to end an argument
is to remove one article
of clothing at a time,
gently tossing it into
your lovers direction
until you resemble Eve
in the garden–
i find it to be quite
hard to
quarrel with that..

come, rest your weary
head on my
shoulders–
for they were built
strong for
things such as this. .

there 's not enough
appreciation
for those who shoulder
the weight
of broken hearts. .

those who claim you to
be anything other than
beautiful,
have a very ugly heart..

..and i shall always
bend the knee
of my heart for those
who are aching—
for i, too,
know what it's like
to bleed alone..

she could spend her
time however
she wanted–
but all she ever
wanted,
was to spend it
with you..

i have always
burned for
everything
i have
ever loved. .

it's all in how well
you hold
their heart when
it 's aching. .

you never had to win
me over–
i have always been
yours. .

i went out on
a quest,
not to find love,
but to understand it;
and with that,
came the knowledge
of all that it wasn't–
and although
that was hard,
i still found that love,
in all of its forms,
was still beautiful. .

i've never understood
why people
stay on the surface
of things,
when everything
beautiful is
hidden in the deep. .

perhaps she just wants
to be
craved a little deeper,
something
a bit more beyond skin?

appreciate those
who take notice
of the little things
that matter you. .

brave is the one who
LOVES,
despite all the
HATE
that surrounds them..

it never really
mattered
where
we went—
the
DESTINATION
was always
LOVE..

..and i would do it all
over again:
lose my way and
fall again,
trip over lessons and
how-not-to be's –
as long as it
leads back to you. .

sometimes,
i feel like we're all
staggering through life:
tripping over feelings,
lessons, and souls;
drunk on the thought
of love,
and simply—
just trying to
find our way home. .

give her something
beautiful to hang on to:
a lifetime full of precious
memories that
she can tuck
underneath her ribs–
because in the end,
that will be what
holds her. .

there was something
different
about him that day,
something
MAGICAL
that i couldn't
place my finger on –
and all i could do was
FALL IN LOVE
with him
ALL OVER AGAIN..

sometimes,
you just want to be
held
for a while and told
pretty things. .

please forgive me,
darling,
if there are times
when i'll need
to hear the words you 've
said a
thousand times,
yet again–
you see,
all i've ever known is
DARKNESS
and your whispers.. well,
they're like a
GENTLE LIGHT
breaking through, and
sometimes,
I NEED THAT..

sometimes,
you just want to
HOLD
on to
THE MEMORIES—
because that 's all that 's
left
holding you. .

you deserve a lover
that goes
to war
with you,
not against you. .

sure,
she's beautiful,
but it goes
way
deeper than skin. .

i hope that
when you find a lover,
that they touch your
soul the way
the sun touches the horizon,
at sunset—
i hope they gently
run their
fingers across all the cracks
and
rough edges,
and simply. .
fall for your darkness. .

she never
asked for much,
just a peaceful,
easy-chair kind of love-
one that she could
nestle into at
the end of a long day
and just..
BE

one day,
you 're going to be sitting
on the couch,
eating popcorn with the
love of your life,
smiling and laughing,
and will have forgotten all
of the sorrow,
that once
stole your smile away. .

words aren 't
always
necessary. .

who knew. .

i watched as she cried,
and I don't mean lightly. .
she wept bitterly.
so much so,
that oceans were created
from her salty
tears.
i watched as she raged,
not angrily,
but with sorrow of heart—
and i marveled at the
fire that shot out
from her nostrils
and at her voice of
thunder that rocked my soul,
as i felt her violently
shake the earth
beneath me—
and the only conclusion
i could come to,
was that the sky,
like me,
had a soul and could feel.
and she, too,
was beautiful for it..

i know nothing more
save how to be
AUTHENTIC —
so, when i'm sad, i 'll cry.
when i'm happy,
a smile will spring
forth,
and when i'm tickled,
always will i
laugh —
so, if your desire is
for me to take
on any other form,
i just cannot —
for i was, am,
and always will be. .
REAL

i think we're all
just looking
for that someone,
who paints a rainbow of
COLORS
inside of
our
darkened hearts. .

WOMAN,
is a man's heart.
MAN,
is the ribs—
the rib cage,
protects the heart—
so, if man crushes woman:
in reality,
he's breaking his own heart..

it hurt, too much,
watching the world
burn each other
to the ground—
so much so,
that she made a
promise to herself
to never be
that person, no matter what—
and so, she loved..
even with tears streaming
down her face,
as they burned their
scars into her soul..
SHE LOVED

i tend to gravitate
towards the
broken things,
the dark and
abandoned people–
for those are the
ones that,
i believe, have been
through the
most hell
and have the highest
degree in understanding. .

you can try to
break her,
but you won 't–
no matter how much
you try,
she '11 just keep
loving
the hell out of you. .

my heart sinks low
as i see those words
written..
the ones in which
so many people
resonate with, so easily. .
and i wonder
if they understand what
it took,
the price that was paid,
the cost of it all..
the light which prevailed
through darkness,
the blood-stained ink
that flowed from the heart,
wetting the tip of the pen
that scribbled out those truths,
just to bring them to the surface. .
I WONDER

all i'll ever know. .
is love,
because all i 've ever known,
was HATE
and why would anyone,
who has ever
known how it feels to be on the
receiving end of that hate,
offer that to another soul?
it is love that cures,
that covers a multitude of sin-
and i don 't think i 'll ever
understand why people insert hate
where love should be-
choice, freedom of that choice,
and yet, they still choose hate-
I WEEP AT SUCH TRAGEDIES

we're all in this
together—
i just wish people
would start acting like it. .

my heart did cry
a thousand
rivers,
my soul did weep
the salty sea,
and when i looked down
into the waters,
it was only but myself
looking back at me—
only then did i learn,
that hell wasn't just
some place
i'd be banished to
for my transgressions
in the afterlife,
but simply,
the absence of a
genuine soul who cared. .

if you can find the
COURAGE
to love
yourself,
all else will fall
into place..

heaven, i feel,
is not some magical place
in the
sky where we go to when
we breathe
our last and die, no.
heaven. .
well, heaven is just a smile,
kindness, compassion,
and care,
offered unselfishly
by a genuine
soul that cares. .

compassion, care, kindness,
thoughtfulness, patience,
warmth,
resolve, respect,
understanding,
listening, connecting,
concern,
encouragement, friendliness. .
all things beautiful
that make up
love–
and all things that
went extinct
with the dinosaurs..

you are allowed
TO FEEL,
and you are also allowed
TO SHARE
those feelings—
I just hope
that when you do,
you have someone
on the receiving end
that cares. .

life is always on a
forward march,
and we are forced
to fall in line–
don't be afraid
to step out of
that sequence,
from time to time,
and stop 🌸
to smell the flowers. .

it is not what you say
that lives on —
it 's all in how
you make people feel. .

some people
can silence your
demons
with just
their presence
alone. .

life has always taught me
how not-to-be-
and for that,
i ' m grateful. .

let your hands be
strong enough to
PROTECT
her and yet,
still gentle enough
to stroke
HER VERY SOUL..

..and if she should
only be
granted just
one more morning rise,
and you had the knowledge
that she
would breathe her last
this very night,
how would you treat her
that day?

DO THAT ALWAYS..

fall in love
with someone who makes
you a priority,
a person
who makes time for you
because you're worth it—
someone who
makes you feel special
and important enough
to get to know,
and grow with.
fall in love
with a heart that wants
to learn
every color of your soul
and why
you bleed the rainbow—
but mostly,
fall for one who,
even when they're angry,
will still look after
and cradled your heart—
one who simply, cares. .

..and i'm still
chasing
BUTTERFLIES,
in a world
where
i'm told to let
go of the
MAGIC
and grow up. .

i don't think i'll ever
understand the world
in which we
live—
where love is exchanged
for hate,
understanding is replaced
by judgment,
and respect..
well, respect is just about
non-existent..

i am but a wildflower
dancing in the breeze,
the one that is
overlooked
and mowed down
as a weed—
but eventually,
they will come to
understand,
that the most beautiful
of flowers
are the wild ones,
you see—
and even if they'11
believe it not,
i 'm still beautiful, to me. .

if you find that someone
who is willing
to do anything for you
come hell or
high water,
a no-matter-what
kind of soul ,
who makes sacrifices
for you, without excuse,
beause they'd rather
take on the
weight just to make your
life a little bit easier-
you should probably
hang on to them
with both hands,
maybe even your legs, too,
because people like that
don't come around often
and if they just so happen to,
you ' ve struck it rich. .
in love, that is. .

find someone
who holds
your ache as if
it were their own. .

words have the power
to CREATE,
and also
to DESTROY-
be careful, oh my soul. .

most of my feelings
are lodged in
drafts,
embedded deep
within
the walls of my chest..

every evening,
you take me back
to the very first night–
where butterflies fluttered,
kisses ran rampant,
and two souls
melded together
in love. .

tell me,
where is it that
the music goes
when the
songbird sings?
i wish to go there. .

when my mind does
wander
to darker things,
and my soul is crushed
by their weight,
it is then that i sit
quietly in nature and let
the birdsongs carry
me back to Eden,
creating a garden of
roses in my mind. .

picking the wounds
from my heart,
in hopes of
making a bouquet
and burning it. .

you are love,
even when mistaken
for all that
isn't–
and if no one
can see that,
believe it for yourself,
because your heart
needs that. .

oh, how she cried
those many tears,
and He caught them,
every one—
because, unlike the others,
to the King,
they were sacred
messages from her soul,
letters written
without hands—
and He molded them,
each tiny tear,
into a vest of armor,
of strength,
and that.. of love..

each time i see a
fresh-cut-flower
in a store,
i think death,
and my heart turns
morbid.
i see a life
that was stripped
from its roots,
without consent,
and a tiny piece of
my heart
turns to soil
just to try
and keep it safe. .

i tip my hat to
all those
who broke me—
i owe you
for helping me become
the strong woman
that i am, today.
so, here's to the haters—
may you be shown
the same
kindness, in return. .

she 's the type of girl
who will
meet you on the
back porch, every night–
with a smile in her eyes,
and love in her heart–
like the very first time,
every time. .

there are beautiful
souls
everywhere,
if you can't find one,
be one –
give what you would
like to receive,
and if you receive
it not,
you will in the life
that is to come. .

i miss the midnight smiles
and the
way you use to look at me.
i miss the moments
when all that
mattered to you was me.
i miss the times
when you use to
breathe life into me. .
i just really miss you,
my heart said to me. .

do not fear those
who weep,
but fear those
who look upon it
and do nothing. .

she was a fighter,
but the gentle kind,
never giving up
in anything because
she didn 't know how to.
she was fashioned
with a heart
built solid on belief that
all would be well,
even if it didn't
feel that way.
and she. .
she was one
that kept you hanging
on to hope,
like it was the breath
that kept you alive–
that woman was
the type of soul that
you wanted in your corner,
for when she said
'she 'd love you until
you breathed your last..
she would

life keeps on moving
forward
and we are pushed to
progress with it.
that requires a certain
growth and change that,
not everyone,
is willing to do.
and there will be times
when you'11 want those
that you love to journey
with you,
but they won't take
the necessary
steps in order to do so.
as much as that hurts,
you can't let that
stop you from
becoming your best
and advancing forward-
in those moments,
just keep moving
and growing with the flow,
and those
who are meant to be there,
will show up. .

i miss the old days,
when people actually
spent quality time
together—
where face met face,
body language gave an
understanding,
and love. .
well, that was something
beautiful ,
shared between
two people alone. .

the only thing
i ever asked love for,
was a best friend.
one who did not fear
the ache they
saw in my heart,
but simply,
chose to hold it as if
it were their own..

..and may the thorns
remind you,
not of pain,
but, of strength,
of growth,
and that sometimes,
it is necessary to bleed. .

do not hide
your struggles just
because a person doesn't
know how to handle them,
or for fear of their
reaction.
we all twinkle,
and we all also dim
at times,
and there's nothing wrong
with that.
you are a real person,
with real feelings
and should not
have to hide
certain parts of your story,
just to make another
comfortable.
just keep on feeling
your way through,
and sharing;
keep on being genuine,
real, and
authentic you –
the right person will hear
you and accept you
as a whole,
not just stick around
for the pretty pieces. .

not always,
does distance make the
heart grow fonder , no.
there are times when
that distance is far
to heavy of a weight
to carry.
it can become a
constant agony,
that rips your heart out.
sometimes, distance is
nothing more than
the absence of love–
and sometimes, that is
your own
personal hell. .

sometimes, there's not
much left to do
save to weep..
and people think that 's
because you ' re
too damn sensitive?
what they don 't realize
is, that 's one of your
best qualities,
that ' s why you love
past your own human nature,
harder than anyone has,
or ever will—
no, you cry because
sometimes, it 's
just too damn much—
and so, you weep. .
you weep at those
who take, and keep on
taking without a
smidgen of give in
their soul—
but you '11 be okay,
you'll always be okay;
and that, my friend,
is what makes you
strong,
and so damn beautiful..

i've always been one to match
energy, so if i'm being 'ugly',
chances are, you are too.
if i am being 'dramatic', chances
are, you're probably putting on
quite the show, yourself–
but i believe i'm done with all
that nonsense–
for if i am only but a mirror, then
i am just the same; and i never much
wanted to be like the multitude,
only myself–
So from now on, if the energy ask
me to rise higher, then with the
occasion shall i ascend–
and may i, with grace, be granted
the strength to do just that. .

what a tragedy,
choosing hate
over love. .

i think
what we all crave,
is a
no-matter-what
kind of soul..

make as many
memories
as you can
because in the end,
that will be
what holds you. .

do not waste your
energy on people
who will never
understand you,
nor even attempt
to try to–
if they wish to
misunderstand you
and be ugly, so be it–
their business, not yours. .

hate or love,
kindness or anger–
some of the most
important
decision of your life..

when i find that my heart is starting
to sink deep into the pits below, i
take a trip into nature-
i pay close attention to the way the
leaves clap their hands to their Maker
when He sends them a warm and gentle
breeze.
i listen to the language of the
cardinal, understanding fully why he is
perched on the fence, staring back at
me.
i take notice of the flowers as they
reverently bow their heads in prayer,
and the green spires of grass that hold
them as they do so, over there.
i feel the cooling of the Earth as it
gently caresses my bare feet,
and suddenly, i discover the quieting
sound of my once, rapid heartbeat. .

you deserve someone who, at the end
of the day, is excited to see you;
a person who just can't seem to get
enough of you.
one who spends time on you and then,
spends some more.
you deserve a love that's
interested in you, a person who
wants to talk and connect with you.
someone who supports your dreams and
encourages you in them.
you deserve a love that simply. .
cares about all of you. .

life is way too short
to be
ANYTHING
other than someone's
EVERYTHING..

all i'll ever need
is the little,
small moments
where the world falls
away
and there's nothing left
but us,
falling into one another. .

romance
will never
go out of style. .

yeah, that woman is a lot to
handle, but that 's only because
she has been through hell and
doesn 't play, nor settle for
anything less than what she knows
she deserves.
she has learned to give herself of
the love she has never received
and isn 't, for one second, afraid
to call people out on their shit—
but that woman will also love you
with a passion and for all the
right reasons;
and she will care for you in every
way she's never been cared for,
for forever, if you' ll let her. .

amazing is not trying
to convince
a person to love you—
no, amazing is
someone that looks
for you and not only that,
but, one who looks at you
like they're the
luckiest soul alive
and reminds you
of that—
and amazing,
well, that is the one
that chooses you,
every single day,
simply because..
they want to..

maybe he does care?
maybe he just doesn't know
how to show it because
his insides are shivering
from the biting
frost of a love gone cold?
maybe if you hold him long
enough, that icy glass will
melt away?
and maybe, just maybe,
he needs
to know what it feels like to
come home to warm hands and
a warm heart,
one that accepts and loves him
as is, without condition?
maybe? ?

don 't ever let her
miss you
for too long.
you may end up
regretting that
when she begins to
enjoy her
own company
because that's just
something that is
really hard
to come back from..

there have been
times
when i have
rested softly
in your arms and
others that
i've collapsed—
but you,
sweet angel of love,
you have held me
either way
and for that,
i'm grateful. .

always
keep a little love
tucked
away in your pockets. .

today,
i wish to be
a river for you,
flowing quietly amidst
the most
beaut iful valley that
hasn't been discovered
by human hands
just yet–
one that is still raw
and brave enough
to love the stones
and yet,
still gentle enough
to care for
the flowers growing
inside your soul..

sometimes,
a woman just wants
you to pull her
in only to be near
her soul,
with no further
intentions. .

i hope
you find
your
wings. .

..and if the moon had
a sound,
it would be him. .

sitting out here,
on the back porch
of a Sunday's
morning rise,
i watch as the breeze
gently runs her
fingers through
the leaves of the trees
and i am reminded
of your soft,
tender touch. .

..and when i 've
breathed my last,
i can only hope
that i have
brought at least
a tiny bit of joy
to your world..

i believe in magic,
in moonlight kisses,
and dancing
in the rain.
i believe in hope
that is given in a
passing smile and the
peace that comes with it,
just the same–
but mostly, i just believe in
HIM..

i hope you don't
mind if i keep
believing
in you for a
lifetime or three? ?

she was
such a delicate creature
but always
fierce at heart–
and he..
he was an angel,
a warrior
sent to love and protect
her for
longer than eternity. .

being a woman
doesn't mean
turning the head
of many men with
flattering lips,
but holding the attention
of one
with your silence alone..

never underestimate
the power of
a SMILE,
and a little dash
of KINDNESS–
hearts are
turned
by such things. .

i don't think
there's enough
ink in life
for all that
my heart
bleeds. .

..and he loved me,
when i had been
banished by the
whole world,
he simply,
took me under his
wings,
and loved me. .

i caught a scent of
jasmine
🌸 wafting
from your soul–
and suddenly,
i loved flowers. .

who says beauty
doesn't last?
if your heart is kind,
you will always
be beautiful. .

i laid down my sword
long ago—
love will fight for me,
and i will remain still. .

she's deep–
i hope
you can swim..

always,
in all ways—
i 'll be loving you. .

you never know
how much a kind
word may mean
to someone–
sometimes,
something as simple
as that can mean the
world to a soul
who is thirsty
of such things, in
a dry and baron land. .

you have me,
in all ways–
ALWAYS

..and if you remember
anything
about them,
remember that it is
but a
privilege to be
a part of their
life–
and treat them well..

you're
ALL HEART,
in a
heartless world–
and that,
is what makes you
so damn beautiful. .

there is something
damn beautiful in
understanding–
to be able to step out
of your own
soul and into another's
for a moment,
to feel what they feel,
and to have the ability
to have an
intelligent and
empathetic response–
that 's intimacy,
that 's love. .

he is my heart—
and there 's
just no walking
away
from that..

if you want to get
your point
across,
ask questions –
it makes people
think,
any there are many
who just don ' t think
to do that. .

come,
my love,
take me back to that
place where you saw me
through the eyes
of love,
when all that i did
made you fall
so deep,
and just..
hold me there..

i learned how
to write—
because i have yet
to find a soul
that actually listens. .

..and if you have ever
felt your
soul ripped out,
bleeding at the seams,
broken pieces scattered
about the land—
well then, i guess you
have loved
with all of your heart,
and there are no
mistakes in that—
you have journeyed well..

grow
with the flow. .

the sweetest thing
in love—
is the falling. .

your smell..
your laugh..
the gentle touch
of your hand..
they all just sort of..
linger

there was love,
and then,
there was your love—
and that,
was entirely different. .

with you,
i finally know
what home feels like. .

some things in life
just become
more precious
when they're given
freely from a heart,
without the
need to ask. .

'as long as you're still smiling.'

Love, Dad

'i love you'
means so much more
when the giver
of those words,
offers up
the little things that
make you,
not just hear,
but feel it. .

give your smile away
and it will
be given back to you. .

if everyone 's soul
was the same
color,
the rainbow wouldn't
be as bright,
nor as beautiful–
so, never allow anyone
to make you feel like
it 's not okay to be
your own unique self. .

you ARE deserving
of kindness.
you ARE
worthy of a heart that
cares about yours.
and you Are
deserving of a soul
who will look upon you
like they would the
morning sunrise. .
with nothing less than
complete amazement..

she was
a beautiful woman
with a whole world
of beautiful
tucked up
under her ribs–
but everyone was
so busy
judging her,
that they failed to
even notice. .

all she ever
really wanted was a
soul that cared–
someone who
was there for her,
not because
she begged them to be,
but simply,
because they wanted to..

tell me where
the wild
things grow,
i wish to join
them in
their peaceful
abode—
where i shall
neither toil,
nor spin,
and dance,
ever so quietly,
with the wind..

the world had all
grown so cold–
you were just about
all the warmth
i had left in my life. .

i ran with the worst
of people:
the forgotten, the hated,
the despised and such-
we took wrong turns
and we did
dumb things,
but i believe that
to be the place
where i learned the
most about life-
jumping off cliffs
and discovering
my wings, acceptance,
and the
turning of the cheek..
but mostly,
learning to love every
single soul for absolutely no
reason at all-
life has been
so very generous to me..
and for that, i' m thankful..

those tears,
sweet angel,
they're taking
your soul to
where it must go..

men are built
differently
than women,
and just because
they don ' t
express their
feelings the same
way we do,
doesn' t mean
they
don 't have any. .

your heart
will
know when
it's
HOME..

..and he always
kisses my
forehead
at the exact
moment i need
it most..

words are so damn
important.
sure, actions are too,
but words. .
oh how those words can
stick around and linger
for longer than
you know.
they come with the power
to settle, and with great
strength to bring
you to your knees—
so please, just be very
careful with what you
put out there. .

in this life,
i hope you have the ability to see
beyond your own thoughts.
i hope your imagination opens up to the
beauty in the people that surround you.
i hope you have the courage to allow
your heart to open wide,
feeling beyond your own emotions,
and sharing in what others experience—
for there is beauty in that kind of
connection,
a certain blessing that lies therein—
for to feel, to connect ,
to experience a soul. .
is to understand—
and that kind of depth is where
friendships are formed that are both
fulfilling and,
most importantly, lasting. .

one day,
she just kind of.. woke up-
she saw that her life was not her own,
that it was being slowly stolen away
from her.
she had always lived and breathed for
others,
doing and saying what other people
wished her to. .
and then, one day,
she finally said, 'no more',
snatching her life back into her own
hands,
no longer allowing others to live
vicariously through her-
for there was only but one life,
and she would live it on her own terms,
her own way. .
and with that, came FREEDOM. .

if you're going to
live this life,
and i mean
really live it,
do it with your all. .

last night,
i told the
moon 🌙
about you:
and all the
trees
bowed their
heads low,
the stars, ✦
and all of
heaven
gathered' round
to quietly
listen. . 🌙

meet me in the moment..

i think one of the
hardest things
i've ever had to do
was to take
all this kindness
and love,
this open, caring heart,
and teach it how not
to give a fuck. .

the air is crisp and
the leaves
are fall, 🍃
fall, 🍂
falling, 🍁
showing us just how
beautiful
that can be..

i stumbled upon
an angel weeping
and saw that her wings
were bent and torn.
so i knelt down there
beside her,
to dry her tired eyes,
and all of a sudden,
without any warning,
her face
turned in to mine..

in those rare
moments
that you bathe in
the raw
and open those
clinched fists,
i will be there
to kiss your
bloody wounds
and soothe the
stinging
ache with endless
song;
and i will hold
you,
with all that
i am,
and never
let go–
FOREVER..

i wish people
had the
ability to see
the world
through each
other 's eyes —
then,
and only then,
would they be
able
to understand
how their
loving,
and
not-so-loving
ways,
shape humanity..

' stay',
she
requested. .

'in a world
where
everyone
leaves,

just stay'. .

as i lay
my head on
your chest,
i discover a
whole other
world, hidden
beneath your
skin:
where there's the
sound of
streams rippling,
bare-branches
creaking
and even the howl
of a
distant wolf
calling my name..

what if sorrow
and pain
were nothing more
than
a silent friend?
what if they were
just
journeying
alongside
you,
holding your hand,
leading you to
comfort
and love–
and simply,
helping you find
your
way home? ?

she loves
nature
and the way it
speaks to her
of how it is
okay to
be full of
details
and yet,
still soft and
delicate
at the same
time..

please forgive me, darling,
for gazing upon you
so often, but when your
eyes met mine, i went
on a journey through
your soul-
staining my lips with soft,
red rose petals and
entwining in the vines, laced
around your heart.
i soaked in the saltiness
of ancient seas, as the
waves and the warmth of
your love washed over me.
i crossed over a bridge,
where waterfalls of
memories cascaded through
your mind, and i was
ignited by a ring of volcanic
fire of pleasant poetry,
surging through your veins
and delight filled my stomach,
as my heart stopped
to recline-
so please forgive me,
sweet love, for gazing at
the sacred stars in your
eyes, but who, after all that,
Couldn't get lost
in a soul that divine? ?

i have so
much love
tucked away
in my
pockets..

some people
stop by for
only a
short time,
and although
that's
necessary,
i'm thankful
for
the ones
that stay..

find
someone
who's not
afraid
of what
forever
takes. .

come,
wrap your soul
around me
and let love
make us..

it's really not
that hard to
please a woman –
all you have to do is
CARE..

a soul collision
so strong
that when one falls
asleep,
the other closes
their eyes..

how rare and lovely
it is
to find someone who,
not only, celebrates
with you in the
good times,
but one that holds you
even tighter
when those moments get
tough, as well..

'i got you'
is
a love language..

i gathered up a bouquet of
memories,
like some gather
wildflowers,
and tied a ribbon
'round them—
gently tucking them
away inside of
my heart,
where they would be safe
until I
needed them again..

i was brave
because i loved. .

one day,
i hope
thy can understand
that
their fight is not
with flesh and
blood–
i hope that brother
can stop
slaying brother,
and love
can return to them all..

do all things with love,
all else
is a tragedy. .

Printed in Germany
by Amazon Distribution
GmbH, Leipzig